The Keys To The Magic

A Play Therapist's Handbook of Family Centered Play Therapy

Anne Maxwell
LCSW, RPT-S

ACCESS
CONSCIOUSNESS®
PUBLISHING

The Keys to the Magic

Copyright © 2013 by Anne Maxwell

ISBN: 978-1-939261-43-4

All rights reserved. No part of this publication may be reproduced, stored in a retrieval system, or transmitted, in any form or by any means electronic, mechanical, photocopying, recording, or otherwise without prior written permission from the publisher.

The author and publisher of the book do not make any claim or guarantee for any physical, mental, emotional, spiritual, or financial result. All products, services and information provided by the author are for general education and entertainment purposes only. The information provided herein is in no way a substitute for medical advice. In the event you use any of the information contained in this book for yourself, the author and publisher assume no responsibility for your actions.

Published by Access Consciousness Publishing, LLC

www.accessconsciousnesspublishing.com

Printed in the United States of America
International printing in the U.K. and Australia
First Edition

About Parenting

"Most people have the idea that good parenting is based on being right versus being wrong. They think it's about getting 'results,' being in control and having all the right answers. They think good parenting is about indoctrinating kids into a certain way of being and trying to make life predictable. The problem with trying to train kids to be normal, real and predictable is that it imposes huge limitations and judgments on them. It does not allow for the greatness of children."

~ Gary Douglas, *Conscious Parents, Conscious Kids*, 2008 ~

The Keys to the Magic

"When two persons meet in a creative relationship, there is a continuing sense of mutuality and togetherness throughout the experience... The whole idea of errors or mistakes in the creative relationship is irrelevant. It is not possible to do right or wrong in such a relationship. It is a matter of being, of presence, of thisness, of a life being lived rather than a matter of individuals being acted upon. All references to responses and their correctness or incorrectness are inappropriate."

~ Clark Moustakas (1959) ~

Acknowledgments

I am so grateful to the many phenomenal people in my life that contributed to the creation of this handbook.

First, to Gary Douglas, the founder of Access Consciousness®, thank you for being the inspiration you are to me. Thank you for your kindness and generosity and knowing. And, thank you for the amazing Access Consciousness® tools, questions and processes that I use on a daily basis and that are woven throughout this handbook.

And, to Dain Heer, co-creator of Access Consciousness®, thank you for being the magic and the gift you are to me and to the kids.

To Bryan Post, LCSW, gratitude for insisting that no one else does the kind of therapy I do and for encouraging me to name it and claim it and write about it and teach it.

To Byron and Carol Norton, Ed. D, thank you for your time and generosity in teaching me about play therapy and giving me a sense of self-confidence in the play therapy room.

To Alicea Lybarger, whose assistance and support over the years have been invaluable.

To Curry Glassell and Tanja Barth, for giving me the final push to complete this handbook.

To my play therapy colleagues, for your enthusiasm and excitement and sparkle! Thank you Lisa Dion, LPC, RPT-S; Anne Watts, LCSW; Mia Bertram, LPC; and Whitney Jose, LPC, RPT-S and so many others.

And especially to the magical and amazing kids and families who have graced my life and from whom I have learned so much.

Thank you all.

Anne Maxwell,
LCSW, RPT-S

CONTENTS

Introduction 1
1 Your Vision 3
2 Play 5
3 Play Therapy 6
4 Family 7
5 Principles of Family Centered Play Therapy 9
6 More about Family Centered Play Therapy 10
7 Role of the Play Therapist 11
8 Role of the Child 13
9 Role of the Parent 14
10 Assessment 16
11 More on Assessment 18
12 Interventions in the Play Therapy Room 21
13 More Interventions 24
14 Termination 28
References 30
About the Author 32
Family Centered Play Therapy Classes 34
Access Consciousness® Seminars, Workshops and Classes 35
Other Access Consciousness® Books 40

The Keys to the Magic
A Play Therapist's Handbook of Family Centered Play Therapy

Introduction

I love working with kids! I love their energy! I love their ability to be present! I love their willingness to heal and to move on! I love their capacity to be catalysts for change in the lives of those whose paths they cross…family members, peers, teachers, coaches and friends! And it doesn't seem to matter what their life experiences have been. It is easy for them to tap into the magic of creation and transformation.

And, something else that I love is their ability and willingness to communicate in so many different ways, in addition to using their words. They communicate energetically. They communicate with their behaviors. They communicate through their play. They communicate using body language.

The Keys to the Magic is the handbook I wish I had been given when I first started working in a professional capacity as a play therapist with kids and families! It is designed to be a reference guide—something that you can turn to when you feel stuck or at a loss. It is practical and is designed to give you a sense of where else you can go with the kids and families with whom you work.

I remember early on, in play therapy sessions when the child would say or do something, and I would find myself at a loss as to how to respond, and, I would panic. This handbook is for those of you who, on occasion, find yourselves there. Today, I use these same tools. I don't always know instantly what to say or do, and, I now have the tools that I can use to tap into whatever is required for that particular child in that particular moment.

The Keys to the Magic is not about finding answers. It's about accessing the magic of you and of the kids and of the two of you together. This handbook is designed to get you out of your logical thinking mind and into the energy that is creating the relationship that you have, or would like to have, with the kids and families with whom you work. It's also about accessing you—and the difference that you are. It's about accessing you being you in the play therapy room with the kids and their parents. It's not about you replicating what anyone else does. What if you could take what you have learned from others that works for you, and, what if you could expand on that by being you and being present and asking questions?

The questions in this handbook are not logical, left-brained questions that are going to give you answers or formulas you can plug in. They are designed to create awareness. They are designed to tap you into what you actually know that you may not have given yourself permission to know. Awareness is knowing. When you ask a question, it gives you a sense of what is. That's awareness. The awareness will give you a sense of what else is possible in the moment and what choices you have available to you. Then, you can choose what to say or do or ask another question, which will give you another awareness…and so on.

And, the questions I ask are not statements with a question mark at the end of them. They are questions that don't have a right answer or a wrong answer. The awareness you have from asking a question opens the door to multiple possibilities—possibilities you may not have known were available. Isn't that more fun than worrying about whether you are getting it right or not?

This handbook also describes the modality of play therapy I have come to call my own. Over the years, my practice has evolved into what I call Family Centered Play Therapy. It is an approach, facilitated by the therapist, in which the child and parent can co-create the connection they would like to have with each other and the way they would like to be with each other. At the invitation of the child, it can include parents, not as co-therapists, but as participants in the play. It is child directed. The child is in charge. Parents may be given various roles by their child and they must do as they are told! And, it is family centered. The family is the client; the child facilitates the parent; the parent facilitates the child.

The magic of this approach is that healing happens so much more quickly and more easily than it does in any of the other modalities I have used, and, from what my clients tell me, it lasts longer.

As I tell my clients, please take the tools that work for you, and, leave the ones that don't! And, please continue to use what has worked for you in the past! This is not about throwing anything away! It is all about letting go of what's not working for you. It's about providing you with a new approach and new tools and processes to assist you as you continue along your path of being you and being a play therapist.

Wishing you many magical moments!   *Anne Maxwell, LCSW, RPT-S*

Chapter 1

Your Vision

"The power of a vision statement is that it gives you clarity and enables you to go outside of what you have already decided is the only thing you can do."

~ Steven Bowman (2010) ~

Here are some questions you can ask yourself.

- Take a moment and jot down what comes to you.
- Keep adding to it.
- Does it change over time?
- What do you notice?

As a play therapist, what is your vision for the children and families with whom you work?

Are you willing to look outside of the way you've decided things should be?

What if your point of view creates your reality? (Heer, 2011)

What if your point of view about yourself, about play therapy, about play, about the families with whom you work actually creates what you see in your families?

Ask yourself: What is the impact I want to have on the children, parents and families I serve?

Ask yourself: What is the difference I would like to make in their lives? (Bowman, 2010)

How do you know if you have a good vision? When it works!!! (Bowman, 2010)

Chapter 2

Play

"For children, toys are words and play is language."

~ Garry Landreth (2002) ~

Some questions for you:

What is play?

What does play mean to you?

What is the language of play?

What are they saying when they play?

Chapter 3

Play Therapy

"An eight-year-old girl suddenly stopped her play and exclaimed, "In here I turn myself inside out and give myself a shake, shake, shake, and finally I get glad all over that I am me."

~ Virginia Axline (1974) ~

What is play therapy?

What does play therapy mean to you?

What is the value of play therapy?

Do toys have meanings, or, is it how they are used and the energy of the play that counts?

Chapter 4

Family

"A family is more than a collection of individuals; it is a system, an organized whole whose parts function in a way that transcends their separate characteristics."

~ Minuchin, Nichols, Lee (2007) ~

What is family?

What does family mean to you?

What's the value of family?

How many points of view do you have about:

- What family is?

- What parents are?

- What children are?

How many of your beliefs, attitudes, values, and morals are based on trying to fit into your family, or on rebelling against your family?

How many of those beliefs, attitudes, values and morals influence your attitude towards your clients?

Who are the members of a family, and, what are their roles?

Which members have priority?

Who teaches whom?

Who knows more?

How much of you did you create in order to validate your family's point of view about who you should be?

Again, does that influence you as a play therapist? In what ways?

Chapter 5

Principles of Family Centered Play Therapy

"Over the years, my practice evolved into what I call Family Centered Play Therapy. It is based on Clark Moustakas' Relationship Play Therapy, Byron and Carol Norton's Experiential Play Therapy, Bryan Post's Family Centered Regulatory Theory, Family Systems Theory, principles of Access Consciousness™ and my own practice wisdom."

~ Anne Maxwell ~

1. The family is the client.
2. All families are unique. Each member of each family is unique.
3. Parents and children are the experts on themselves and on their families.
4. Healing occurs in relationship.
5. Young children communicate easily through play.
6. Behavior is a form of communication.
7. People do the best they can with the information and tools they have available to them at the time.
8. All negative behavior arises from an unconscious state of stress. When stressed, children (and parents) regress emotionally. (Forbes & Post, 2006)
9. Family Centered Play Therapy sessions are led by the child, for the most part. Parents' needs, fears, concerns are addressed directly, in separate sessions.
10. The therapist's role is:
    - to facilitate communication between child and parent;
    - to facilitate greater awareness on the part of family members of the dynamics within their family; and,
    - to encourage family members to find their respective voices in ways that ensure that they are heard.

Chapter 6

More about Family Centered Play Therapy

"It is a process, facilitated by the therapist, in which the child and parent can co-create the connection they would like to have with each other and the way they would like to be with each other."

~ Anne Maxwell ~

It includes parents, not as co-therapists or "psychotherapeutic agents," but as participants in the play.

It is child directed. The child is in charge. Parents may be given various roles by their child and they must do as they are told!

It is family centered. The family is the client; the child facilitates the parent; the parent facilitates the child.

It is based on the relationship between the child and the parent, and, it is attuned to the connection between the child and parent and to what they would like to have as their relationship.

By teaching parents the language of play, it is designed to facilitate greater communication between parent and child.

By encouraging each to find their own voice, it enables them to speak so that they can be heard.

It is designed to promote greater awareness of each other that comes from the reciprocity of their interactions in the play therapy setting.

It is experiential. Children want to communicate the experience of what it's like to be living their life. (Norton and Norton, 2002) By including parents in the room (at the child's discretion), parents are given that experience, through their child's play.

It facilitates awareness on the part of parents that they might not have otherwise.

It intensifies the process of healing, not only for the child, but for the parent and the family. It speeds up the process dynamically! It can be so much fun!!!

Chapter 7

Role of the Play Therapist

"During the first session of play therapy...a child will communicate to the therapist, 'Here's how life is treating me. Here's my state of being."

~ Byron and Carol Norton (2002) ~

The Play Therapist:

Gives child and parent permission to be who they are.

Encourages child and parent to know what they know.

Trusts her knowing.

Takes her lead from her clients.

Facilitates change to the extent that clients are willing.

Facilitates communication between child and parent, by teaching the language of play to parents.

Is not in search of answers! Instead asks questions, to see what is else might be possible.

When feeling stuck or unsure, asks another question (to herself!):

- What is this?
- What can I do with it?
- Can I change it?
- How can I change it?
- What is the child saying? What does she want us to know?
- What's being communicated by the parent?

Gives full credit to child and parent.

Acknowledges the awarenesses that child and parent have in the session.

Does not give opinions!

Is in allowance of them and their choices. Does not judge:

- Self.
- Child.
- Parent.
- Family.
- Choices they might make.
- Choices they have made.
- Choices they are making.

Meets the child/parent where they are, not where the therapist is.

Communicates with them where they are, not where the therapist knows they could be or wishes they were.

Offers them the possibility of moving beyond where they are and have been, so that they can connect more easily with each other.

Chapter 8

Role of the Child

"Each child is unique, and, in the exact sense, his play differs from every other child. Each child has his own way of expressing himself and his own style."

~ Clark Moustakas (1959) ~

The Child:

Sets the rules.

Expresses himself in his own way and style.

Chooses the toys and activities with which he would like to play.

Assigns roles and play for other participants.

Decides the degree to which others in the room participate.

Is in charge. Is the boss!

Facilitates awareness on the parts of parents and therapist.

Takes on any role he chooses in the moment.

Determines the pace and intensity of the therapy.

Is never "wrong."

Has permission to be who he is.

Is acknowledged for his awareness and for what he knows by therapist and parent.

Chapter 9

Role of the Parent

"While it's not exactly a revelation that kids do better when they enjoy strong relationships with their parents, what may surprise you is what produces this kind of parent-child connection. It's not how our parents raised us, or how many parenting books we've read. It's actually how well we've made sense of our experiences with our own parents and how sensitive we are to our children that most powerfully influence our relationship with our kids, and therefore how well they thrive."

~ Dan Siegel, M.D. (2011) ~

The Parent:

Follows child's lead.

Is attentive to child and play—no reading, texting, nodding off, etc.!

Responds to child; for the most part, does not initiate topics or conversation.

Takes on the roles that their child has assigned, and, verbalizes what it's like to be in that role, i.e., "I don't know if I'll ever be able to learn to follow the rules, because they keep on changing."

Sample roles, assigned to parents by children:

- Observer.
- Silent participant.
- Active participant.
- Comforter.
- Aggressor.
- Protector.
- Cohort.
- Seeker of revenge.

Does not bring up topics. For example, does not say things like: "Joey, did you tell Anne about what happened over the weekend?"

Does not volunteer opinions or comments on the play, for example: "You can't do that! I can't believe you are doing that!"

When given a role and asked to participate, does not withdraw from the play and say, "No, I'm not going to do that." Can refuse to do something, if the refusal falls in line with the play, i.e., "No, I'm not going to brush my teeth… you can't make me!"

Never withdraws from the play and never asks their child, "Why are you doing that?"

Chapter 10

Assessment

"Immediate, magical connections awakened between us, not only with individual children but with the entire group...I witnessed directly the child's powers and resources for problem solving and for shaping and directing life rather than being determined by it."

~ Clark Moustakas (1997) ~

The Practicalities:

Usually begins with parents, before meeting with child. Typically takes place over more than one session, initially with parents.

Paperwork is completed re: disclosure, releases, demographic information, etc.

First question asked to parents: "If you could get anything out of this session to take home with you, what would it be?"

Assessment is ongoing, with parents and with child.

I do a genogram! Always! Great visual aid regarding family connections. Can shed light on lots of who, what, where, when, why and how questions.

Assessment sessions can give parents hope that things can change.

Doing assessment gives therapist a sense of where family members are and what's possible for them.

Process gives therapist awareness of what the child's life has been like, and is.

Parents' points of view about themselves, their children, their marriage, their own upbringing, what's possible for them and their children become evident.

Gives the therapist a sense of what parents can receive and can't receive, what they can hear and can't hear.

Is a vehicle for establishing a therapeutic relationship with parents, in which they can feel heard and understood and not judged.

Treatment goals are set. For example, when parents say "he won't be so angry," I ask them what that means to them, and they are able to shift into the space of what it is like when he is not so angry, and what might be possible for him—and for them—when the anger dissipates.

Behavioral goals are described in terms of frequency, intensity and duration.

Chapter 11

More on Assessment

"Show up with your training, your tools and your awareness; function from a space of no judgment; and, allow them to show you where to go."

~ Dain Heer (2011) ~

First questions:
- If you could get anything out of this session, what would it be?
- If you could get anything out of this work together, what would it be?

Be open to receive what comes in the door! Get rid of any preconceived notions you might have about who, what, where, when, why and how the session will go, has to be, must look like, had better be…

Ask lots of questions of yourself:
- What can they hear?
- Is now the time?
- Where else could I go that I didn't think I was going?
- What questions could I ask here that would change all of this?
- What have I not asked yet that my clients would like to tell me?

Ask lots of questions of your clients:
- What do you know about ___?
- And…what else do you know? And…what else? And…what else?
- How's that working for you?
- Would you be willing to let go of ___ ?
- What's the value of ___?
- What's the value of not ___ ?
- What does ___ mean to you?
- What does not ___ mean to you?

Be willing to be imperfect.

BE PRESENT. If you are totally present, you will always know what your client requires! When you are present, you:

- Don't judge them or yourself.
- Give them permission to be who they are and to choose what they choose.
- Notice what they have got going for them that is working for them.
- Have no point of view about their choices.

Be willing to receive everything they say/give to you...the good, the bad and the ugly.

What do you look for in an assessment with parents?

- I look for the energy that underlies whatever the behaviors are/whatever is going on.
- What is their point of view?
- Where are they stuck?
- What are the roles of family members? Who have they been assigned to be? By whom?
- Who requires those roles?
- What roles have been passed down through the generations?
- What "issues" are significant?
- What fantasies do they have about what has to happen before things work out, i.e., "I'll be happy when..."
- What are the patterns they repeat over and over again despite the fact that what they are doing doesn't work?
- What are they willing to receive?
- What kind of change are they willing to have?
- What are all the ways/excuses they use to avoid that?
- Does anyone have permission to be who they are, or do they align and agree or resist and react to other family members' points of view about them?
- In this family, what are the rewards/punishments for being who you are?
- Is there a catalyst for change within the family? (A catalyst, according to the Oxford dictionary, is a "person or thing that precipitates an event.") Who is the catalyst for change in the family?

- Is there more than one?
- In these 10 seconds, what are parents available for?
- Can that be expanded? What could that look like? When?
- What contribution are the parents to their child?
- What contribution is their child to them?

What do you look for in an assessment with the child?
- I look for the energy with which he makes his first contact with me.
- Where is he?
- What would he like?
- Is she resisting?
- Is he relieved?
- Is she playful?
- Is he cautious?
- Is she shut down?
- Is she trying to please?
- Does she connect with me? How?
- Does she include her parents? In what ways?
- What does she know?
- What would she like me to know?
- What would he like his parents to know?
- What contribution is he to his parents?
- Who is he, underneath all the trauma/drama/emotions/feelings/behaviors?
- What is his role in his family? Was it given to him? By whom?
- Is she willing to be different?
- Is she willing to be who she is? If not, where is she stuck? By whom?
- When does she light up?
- What change would she like?

Chapter 12

Interventions in the Play Therapy Room

"Encouragement helps clients believe in themselves and develop self-efficacy and the "can-do" spirit."

~ Nystul (1999b) ~

To the child, at the first session, I say:
- "In here, you are the boss! That means I will never make you talk about things you don't want to talk about; I will never make you play with things you don't want to play with. When you are in here, you are the boss! That means you are in charge!"
- "Also, if you would like your Mom/Dad in the room, they will be there; if not, they won't."
- And, that's ok."
- "You can invite anyone of us to play with you, or you may play by yourself. It is your choice."

To the parent, before the first session, I:
- describe how different it is in the therapy room, with the child in charge, and parents following his lead;
- remind them not to initiate conversation;
- ask them to be present;
- encourage them to see the world through their child's eyes;
- suggest that they pay attention to their responses to the play;
- encourage them to enjoy the time together, to be grateful for their child's willingness to expose himself to them, and for all the possibilities that can come from this experience.

To the child, in the play:
- I wait to be invited;
- I match her energy;

- I take on any role I am given;
- I respond as if the experience was real: ("Make it stop"; "I can't do anything right"; "I'm so confused"; "Noooooooo", etc.)
- If I am unsure of my role, I will ask for clarification (i.e., "Am I a nice mom or a mean mom?")
- I will translate to the child what the parent has said (i.e., "I know that Mommy says she is crying because she loves you so much. She does love you, and, I wonder if she is crying because she wishes she could change all of this and she thinks she can't right now and she doesn't know how to say that.")
- I will translate to the parent what the child is saying (i.e., "What if he wishes it weren't such hard work? What if he knows how much easier it could be for all of you?")

I do not:
- Ask: "Why are you…?" Ever!
- Say: "Good job!" Instead, I might say: "Wow, how awesome is…! How did you do/make that?" "I love watching you build things, draw, put on a play, etc."
- Try to "fix" anything they might tell me about or do. Instead, I might ask them what they know about it. Also, I will acknowledge whatever it is they are telling me.
- Talk a lot. I am not "wordy." I pay more attention to the experience of being with them, and I follow their lead.

To parents in the play therapy room:
- I'll ask them what it's like to have the experience their child just gave them (changed the rules without warning; yelled at them for doing what they were told to do; left them behind, etc.)
- I'll suggest that they do what their child (without words) is asking them to do, i.e., cuddle him, pick him up, swaddle him, feed him the bottle as if he were a baby, etc.
- I will translate to the parents what the child is saying to them, that they might not hear initially. (i.e., "I wonder if she is telling you she is fine, even though things look so bad, and, she wants you to know that you can be fine too.")

How to end a play therapy session:
- With most children, 20 minutes before it's time to end the session, I say to them: "In 5 minutes, it's going to be time for us to say good bye today." (I want to know that they took in the information, but I don't ask them to acknowledge verbally…you can tell whether they heard you or not, and that's all you need to know.)
- 5 minutes later, I repeat what I said.
- 5 minutes later, I say: "In a couple of minutes, it's going to be time for us to say good bye today."
- A couple of minutes later, I say: "It's time for us to say good bye."
- I remind them that the toys will be waiting for them when they return, and, I recite the list of toys they may have played with, ending with: "All of them are going to be waiting for you when you come back."
- DON'T COUNT DOWN! It agitates most kids.

Chapter 13

More Interventions

Step into the space of you, with no judgment, in total allowance, and say: "Hi!" "Welcome!" Be the space that would allow the limitations to dissolve! Be a catalyst for change.

"As a catalyst for change, anything that is willing to change can and anything that isn't won't, and, you don't have to try to control it to make it happen."

~ Gary Douglas, founder of Access Consciousness® ~

Stop judging you and stop judging your clients!

When you have a judgment about something or someone, nothing can show up in your universe that does not match that judgment.

- Judgment creates separation.
- Judgment eliminates awareness.
- Judgment creates more of what you are judging.
- Anytime someone judges you, it's because they are being it or doing it.
- Anytime you judge someone else, it's because you are being or have been it, or, are doing or have done it.
- Conclusions, standards, answers, limitations and structures keep you stuck.
- Positive and negative judgments are equally insidious.
- Next time you find yourself judging someone or something, try turning it into a question.

Difference between awareness and judgment—It's the energy.

Awareness is light; can change; is mutable with the circumstances. Judgment keeps you locked into whatever it is; constricts; is heavy.

First step is to be aware of what is, not what you wish it were.

Tool: Interesting point of view I have this point of view.

Say it for every point of view you have. "I can't work with this Dad; he reminds me too much of my Dad." Interesting point of view I have this point of view. When you see it's just a point of view and not a truth, you could begin asking questions, and, other possibilities can show up. "What's another way I could be with this?" Another example: "I need an hour to complete this treatment plan." That's an interesting point of view. Then: "I wonder what I can get done in 10 minutes."

You can use this phrase for anything you say/think, and, you can also use it for anything anybody tells you. What if everything was an interesting point of view and not right or wrong?

Tool: Who does this belong to?

This idea is based on the possibility that up to 98% of all our thoughts, feelings and emotions aren't actually ours. What if that's true? Some people think this is bizarre: they say: "What do you mean it's not mine, this thought in my head? This emotion is actually in my body; I am sad. Or, I do think that this is a good idea." If you ask: Who does this belong to? Is this mine or someone else's? You might begin to see that you actually do pick up on other people's thoughts, feelings and emotions.

This is all about energy and our ability to pick up on energy in the world. For example, when somebody walks into the room and they are in a terrible mood, they don't have to say anything for you to know that. We all have the ability to perceive energy. If you don't acknowledge it, you might think that you are the one who is flustered.

So many therapists are convinced that they are nervous about meeting with parents. What if they are picking up on the nervousness of parents—trepidation about therapy, their child, etc? The next time you get nervous, you could ask: Who does this belong to? And if it lightens up at all, or your body gets a little lighter or more at ease, it's not yours. You will still perceive the sensation, but you can say: This is not mine! Thank you for the information!

Then, you could ask:
- "What if my job is to put my clients at ease?"
- What if your job was to quell those fears and to say: "Hi! We're fine!"
- Could that change your relationship with your clients?

Tool: Ask questions. Lots of questions! Of you! Of your clients! While you are in the session!

Do not look for an answer! When you ask a question and you don't try to figure out an answer, your universe expands! Every time you reach a conclusion, you shut off possibilities.

When you ask questions, you change the energy.

These questions are designed to stir up the energy of whatever is keeping you/them stuck, so that there can be more awareness, so that more becomes possible. And remember, a question is not a statement with a question mark at the end! A question is a question! Unlike when you are in school, in these sessions, you don't ask a question to get an answer. You ask a question to get a sense of what is. Asking a question does not presuppose a result. It means asking it from wonderment and with no investment in the outcome. For example, "What do you want for dinner?" is not a question. It is a statement with a question mark at the end of it. It presupposes (a), that the person is hungry, (b), that the person plans on eating, and, (c) that the eating will be in the form of dinner. "Are you hungry?" is a question.

- Who am I being right now (i.e., being unsure)? If I were being me, who would I be?
- What do I know (about this client) that I am pretending not to know or denying I know that if I would acknowledge it, could change everything?
- Who are you being right now? And if you were being you, who would you be?
- What do you know (about your child…) that you are pretending not to know or denying that you know, that if you would acknowledge it, could change everything?
- What's the value of being…(a good parent)?
- What's the value of not being…(a good parent)?
- What's the value of being nervous?
- What's the value of being not nervous?
- What is this? What can I do with it? Can I change it? How can I change it?
- What else is possible?

Tool: Acknowledge the change people do choose, not what they don't choose.

I acknowledge what they tell me, directly and indirectly. I don't fix it or talk them out of it or into something else.

Tool: Be present.

If you are totally present, you will always know what your clients require. Being present is:
- Having no projections or expectations or judgments about them, their choices, etc.
- Not judging them or you.
- Giving them permission to be who they are.
- Noticing what they have got going for them that is working for them.
- Having no point of view about them or their choices.

Tool: Receive everything.

Receive the good, the bad and the ugly!

Tool: Wondering.

I wonder what will happen! I wonder who I'm going to be in this session! I wonder who will show up!

Tool: Be willing to let go of everything you were and they were yesterday and will be tomorrow.

Be willing to let go of any projections and expectations into the future you might have. Also, be willing to let go of any significance you might attach to the past. What if the past is simply information that tells you how they got to be where they are?

Chapter 14

Termination

"In relationship therapy, the child determines the length of time and number of sessions needed to come to terms with issues and problems of living connected with self, others, home or school."

~ Clark Moustakas (1997) ~

Ways to tell when child and parents and family are ready to move on:
- They tell you so.
- They do so.
- The treatment goals have been met.
- They have more ease together.
- The play becomes less pressured.
- Finding something to play with becomes a bit of a chore.
- There are fewer complaints.
- Children spontaneously share experiences in their lives with me...what it was like, how they handled the situation. They share what's working and what's not, and, when they talk about what's not, they describe how they manage it all.
- Parents describe to me issues that came up and how they handled them, and, no longer seek my approval or advice.
- Child and parent have greater confidence in themselves and in their ability to handle their lives.
- Child and parent feel heard and understood by each other.
- Although the behaviors that precipitated treatment may not have disappeared, they are much less intrusive and are more easily dealt with.

Over the course of the treatment, I ask many questions I used to save for termination.
- "Is this helping?"

- "What's different about you?
    - your child?
    - your relationship?
    - your marriage?"
- "What's it like in your home now?"
- "How is it with school? Daycare? Friends? Siblings?"

Sometimes it's not required to have an official termination. Sometimes clients go from weekly sessions to monthly sessions, then cancel and don't call for weeks or months. They might call again, if something else comes up.

References

Access True Knowledge Foundation (2008).
Conscious Parents, Conscious Kids,
Brisbane, Australia: Access LLC.

Axline, V. M. (1974).
Play Therapy,
New York, NY: Random House.

Bowman, S. (Speaker).(2010),
Master Class with Steven Bowman (Video Recording).
Mooloolaba, Australia.

Forbes, H. T. & Post, B. B. (2006),
Beyond consequences, logic, and control: a love based approach to helping attachment-challenged children with severe behaviors (vol. 1).
Orlando, FL: Beyond Consequences Institute, LLC.

Heer, D., Dr. (2011).
Being You, Changing the World,
United States of America: Big Country Publishing.

Landreth, G. L. (2002).
Play Therapy, the Art of the Relationship (2nd ed.).
New York, NY: Brunner-Routledge.

Minuchin, S., Nichols, M. P., & Lee, W-Y. (2007).
Assessing Families and Couples; From Symptom to System,
Boston, MA: Pearson Education, Inc.

Moustakas, C. E. (1959).
Psychotherapy with Children, the Living Relationship,
Greeley, CO: Carron Publishers.

Moustakas, C. E. (1997).
Relationship Play Therapy,
Plymouth, UK: Rowman & Littlefield Publishers, Inc.

Norton, C. C. & Norton, B. E. (2002).
Reaching Children Through Play Therapy: An Experiential Approach (2.ed.).
Denver, CO: White Apple Press.

Nystul, M. (1999b).
Problem-solving counseling: Integrating Adler's and Glasser's theories.
In R. Watts & J. Carlson (Eds.), *Interventions and strategies in counseling and psychotherapy* (pp. 31–42).
Philadelphia: Taylor & Francis.

Siegel, D. J. & Bryson, T. P., (2011).
The Whole-Brain Child,
New York, NY: Delacorte Press.

About the Author

Anne Maxwell, LCSW, RPT-S, is a child and play and family therapist and an Access Consciousness® facilitator. Known as the "Play Lady" by many of the children with whom she works and as the "Kid Whisperer" by some of her colleagues, she facilitates Access Consciousness® workshops worldwide.

Born in Washington, D.C., Anne travelled and lived in Europe as a child. Raised in a bilingual home, she has always known that different is simply different, not right, not wrong.

Anne was trained traditionally as a therapist with specialties in child and play and family therapies. She has over 20 years of experience working with kids of all ages and with all kinds of adults and families. She has been trained by some of the very best in her field and, has worked in a variety of settings, including residential, day treatment, inpatient, day hospital, in home and outpatient.

Prior to working with children and families directly, she worked in Washington, D.C., in national politics. She successfully lobbied for the authorization of and funding for a $25 million primary prevention and early intervention program for at-risk mothers and their babies. Eager to work with children and families, she changed direction from lobbying on behalf of kids and families to attending graduate school, to become credentialed to work directly with them in a clinical capacity.

Knowing that there was more to children than her training led her to believe, she discovered Access Consciousness®, which gave her the tools and processes to enhance what she had learned. In 2010, she founded the Child and Family Play Therapy Center, which is dedicated to empowering kids and parents to know what they know and to create the kind of change in their lives they would like to have. Her practice has evolved over the years into what she calls Family Centered Play Therapy.

Anne now travels the world facilitating classes and has developed a unique approach that teaches kids and parents to tap into and recognize their own abilities and knowing. The results have been magical, phenomenal, amazing! Healing and change are so much easier, more effective, more fun, and faster!

To find out more, please visit:

- www.creatingaconsciousworld.com/leaders/annemaxwell/
- www.annemaxwell.accessconsciousness.com
- www.childfamilyplaytherapy.com

Scan for more information

Play Therapy Workshops

Family Centered Play Therapy – The 10 principles of Family Centered Play Therapy are reviewed. Participants will learn how to do Family Centered Play Therapy assessments and interventions.

Including Parents in the Play Therapy Process – This workshop explores the role of parents in the play therapy process—how to include them and integrate them. Also, we look at the influence our own points of view have on our work.

Use of Self in the Play Therapy Process – As a therapist, do you include yourself in the therapy process? What if you can trust what you know, even if it flies in the face of what you've been told? What if you being you is your most valuable asset in the play therapy process?

Access Consciousness® Core Classes

If you liked what you read in this book and are interested in attending Access seminars, workshops or classes, then for a very different point of view, read-on and sample a taste of what is available. These are the core classes in Access Consciousness®.

Access Bars™
Facilitated by Certified Access Bars Facilitators worldwide

The first class in Access Consciousness® is The Bars. Did you know there are 32 points on your head, which when gently touched, effortlessly and easily release the thoughts, ideas, beliefs, emotions and considerations you have stored in any lifetime?

Is your life not yet what you would like it to be? You could have everything you desire (and then some!) if you were willing to receive more and do a little less! Receiving or learning The Bars will allow this—and so much more—to show up for you!

The Bars class is a prerequisite for all Access Consciousness® Core Classes, as it allows your body to process and receive with ease all the changes you are choosing.

Duration: 1 day

Access Foundation
Facilitated by Certified Access Facilitators worldwide

After the Access Bars, this two-day class is about giving you the space to look at your life as a different possibility.

Unlock your limitations about embodiment, finances, success, relationships, family, YOU and your capacities, and much more!

Step into greater possibilities for having everything you truly desire in life as you learn tools and questions to change anything that's not working for you. You also learn a hands-on body process called Cellular Memory that works wonders on scars and pains in the body! If you could change anything in your life, what would it be?

Prerequisites: Access Bars
Duration: 2 days

Access Level 1
Facilitated by Certified Access Facilitators worldwide

After Access Foundation, Level 1 is a two-day class that shows you how to be more conscious in every area of your life and gives you practical tools that allow you to continue expanding this in your day-to-day! Create a phenomenal life filled with magic, joy and ease and clear your limitations about what is truly available for you.

Discover the 5 Elements of Intimacy, create energy flows, start laughing and celebrating living and practice a hands-on body process that has created miraculous results all over the world!

Prerequisites: Access Foundation
Duration: 2 days

Access Levels 2 & 3
Facilitated Exclusively by Gary Douglas (Founder of Access Consciousness®) and Dr. Dain Heer

Having completed Level 1 and opened up to more awareness of you, you start to have more choice in life and become aware of what choice truly is. This four-day class covers a huge range of areas, including the joy of business, living life for the fun of it, no fear, courage and leadership, changing the molecular structure of things, creating your body and your sexual reality, and how to stop holding on to what you want to get rid of! Is it time to start receiving the change you've been asking for?

Prerequisites: Access Bars, Foundation and Level 1
Duration: 4 days (2 days for Level 2 & 2 days for Level 3)

Access Body Class
Facilitated by Access Body Class Facilitators worldwide

During this three-day class you will learn verbal processes and hands-on bodywork that unlock the tension, resistance, and dis-ease of the body. Do you have a talent and ability to work with bodies that you haven't yet unlocked? Are you a body worker (massage therapist, chiropractor, medical doctor, nurse) looking for a way to enhance the healing you can do for your clients? Come play with us and begin to explore how to communicate and relate to bodies, including yours, in a whole new way.

Prerequisites: Access Bars
Duration: 3 days

Advanced Access Body Class with Gary Douglas

This class offers a unique set of new body processes that give your body the possibility of going beyond the limitations of this reality. What if you could undo the limitations locked into your body that create an alteration of the way it functions? What if your body could become far more efficient? What if you and your body didn't have to function the way everyone in this reality believes they have to?

What if food, supplements and exercise have almost nothing to do with how your body truly functions? What if you could have ease, joy and communion with your body far beyond what is considered possible right now? Would you be willing to explore the possibilities?

Prerequisites: Access Bars, Foundation, Levels 1, 2 & 3 &
the 3-day Access Body Class two times
Duration: 3 days

3-Day Energetic Synthesis of Being Class with Dr Dain Heer

This class is your invitation to come and play with the universe.

In this class, Dain works on one person in front of the group—and on everyone in the room—at the same time. During this time, your being, your body and the earth are invited to energetically synthesize in a way that creates a more conscious life and a more conscious planet.

You will discover that you can become a gift to the planet by being the energies of caring, nurturing, honoring, allowance and gratitude. By being these energies, by being you, you change everything; the planet, your life and everyone you come into contact with. What else is possible then?

Open doors to change, to awareness, and to a universe of oneness and consciousness.

Duration: 3 days
Prerequisites: Access Bars, Foundation & Levels 1, 2 & 3

Energetic Synthesis of Being – The Beginning
with Dr Dain Heer

During this beginning class, Dain will give participants a taste of what is possible in the three-day Energetic Synthesis of Being intensive.

3½ Day Being You, Changing the World Class
with Dr. Dain Heer

There is only one thing you were born to do. You were born to be YOU. Not the "you" your partner, your society or your parents want you to be. It isn't about being successful or *doing* anything better. It is about *being* YOU!

What if you, being you, is all it takes to change everything: your life, everyone around you and the world?

This class presents the possibility of implementing deeply penetrating tools to effect profound change in your life. It's easy to do—all that is required of you is a willingness to ask for and choose to be the truth of you.

Together with the group, you'll explore the very energies of living. You'll get tangible, practical and transformative tools that will allow you to start finding out what is true for you and access your knowing of who you truly BE.

Duration: 3½ days

Being You, Changing the World – The Beginning
with Dr. Dain Heer

This one-evening class, which is open to everyone, will give you a taste of what else is possible in your life. It is also the beginning of the 3½ Day Being You, Changing the World Class.

Access Consciousness® 7-Day Events

Are you an adventurer and a seeker of ever-greater possibilities? Are you willing to consider questions you've never asked before? And are you ready to receive more change than you can imagine? If so, the 7-day event just might be for you!

These invitation-only, freeform classes are held twice a year in beautiful locations around the world by Access Consciousness founder, Gary Douglas. To be invited, you must have attended at least one Level 2 & 3 class in person.

There is no other class or event like this offered anywhere in the world. It is a unique and life-changing experience.

Prequisite: Level 2 and 3
Duration: 7 days

See www.accessconsciousness.com
Scan for more information

Other Access Consciousness® Books

Conscious Parents Conscious Kids
This book is a collection of narratives from children immersed in living with conscious awareness. Wouldn't it be great if you could create the space that would allow your kids to unleash their potential and burst through the limitations that hold them back? To create the ease, joy and glory in everything they do and to consciously take charge of their own lives? *By Gary M. Douglas and Dr. Dain Heer.*

Would You Teach a Fish to Climb a Tree?
A Different Take on Kids with ADD, ADHD, OCD and Autism. People tend to function from the point of view that there is something wrong with these children because they don't learn the way the rest of us do. The reality is that they pick things up in a totally different manner. This book takes a look at that and so much more! *By Anne Maxwell, Gary M. Douglas, and Dr. Dain Heer.*

Being You, Changing the World
Have you always known that something COMPLETELY DIFFERENT is possible? What if you had a handbook for infinite possibilities and dynamic change to guide you? With tools and processes that actually worked and invited you to a completely different way of being? For you? And the world? *By Dr. Dain Heer.*

Divorceless Relationships
A Divorceless Relationship is one where you don't have to divorce any part of you in order to be in a relationship with someone else. It is a place where everyone and everything you are in a relationship with can become greater as a result of the relationship. *By Gary M. Douglas.*

Magic. You Are It. Be It.
Magic is about the fun of having the things you desire. The real magic is the ability to have the joy that life can be. *By Gary M. Douglas and Dr. Dain Heer.*

www.accessconsciousness.com

www.ingramcontent.com/pod-product-compliance
Lightning Source LLC
Chambersburg PA
CBHW011211190426
43197CB00044B/2942